M000028353

Incomplete Maps

Incomplete Maps

Stories contoured by poetry

Judy R. Sebastian

ASHOKA TREE
PUBLISHING

Oregon, USA

2021

Copyright ©2021 Judy Sebastian

Written and illustrated by Judy R. Sebastian

All rights reserved, including the right of reproduction in whole or in part in any form. No part of this book may be reproduced, or stored in a retrieval system, or transmitted in any form or by any means, electronic, mechanical, photocopying, recording, or otherwise, without express written permission of the author.

Library of Congress Control Number 2021912870

ISBN 978-0-578-93165-4

Published in the United States by Ashoka Tree Publishing
info@ashokatreepublishing.com

Author contact:
hello@judyrsebastian.com

In Dedication

To the ones who refuse to give up.
To the ones who look longingly at yesterday.
To the ones who are afraid to wake up.
To the ones who are stuck in action replay.

To the ones who are coping.
To the ones who are grieving.
To the ones who are hurting.
To the ones who are surviving.

I give you these thoughts and desires.
I give you these stories shared around campfires.
I give you these incomplete maps
drawn by the frayed hands of,

us Explorers.
Us Guides.
Us Pilgrims.
Us Pioneers.
Us Settlers.

In Gratitude

To Alphonsa and George,
for being my roots and branches.
For being my rain and sunshine. For bearing me, your fruit.

To Kevin and Masha,
family by blood.
Family by choice.

To Mama and Papa,
whose lessons continue to shape me.
I have so much more to learn. I hope the stars are treating you well.

To Carol and Mike,
for your love.
For your kindness.

To She Pat and He Pat,
for being my most favorite Aunt and Uncle.
For inspiring me in more ways than you know.

To Durian (DSK),
For the kind encouragement.
For believing in my abilities, long before I could I believe in them.

To Palwinder,

for the weekly shawarma reminders.

For the steadfast faith in *Ramia*, and my art.

To Aparna,

my kindred spirit.

Miles away. Close to my heart.

To Lakshmi,

my little *vathe*,

I will forever be your *Kovai Kutti*.

To Anjana (Anju),

Mother of The White Dragon. Mother to my darling godson.

For giving the future, a beautiful future.

To Dr. Thomas,

also lovingly known as Sherin.

For the long, short, and medium conversations.

To Ishani,

for unknowingly showing me what it means to forgive,

heal, grow, and pave the way for others to follow.

To Azam,

for the gift of loyalty. For your honesty.

You will make a wonderful godfather, indeed.

To Christopher,

for the adventures. For stepping up – always.

I'm honored to be your *brosef.*

To Anusree,

how can I compare you to a flower,

when you are an entire garden?

To John,

I saved the best for last – like dessert.

For being my Gray in this Black or White world.

For forcing me to join you on your evening walks.

Yes, you were right. I needed it.

For the gentle squeeze every time you hold my hand.

For tolerating my (self-declared) award-winning jokes.

More so, for loving me

on days when it was hard for me,

to love.

Table Of Contents

Part 1 – The Explorer

The Rebirth Of The Tulip

Dormant under the white powdery blanket.
Waiting in silence. Waiting in patience.
It's quite dark. It's terribly cold.
It's perplexing how it feels both new and old.

Seasons change. The cold blanket melts.
It quenches the appetite of the curious roots.
Fighting the darkness. Fighting the dirt.
The blind shoots break free from the cold earth.

Behold the sun! Behold the sky!
The sights. The sounds. A riot to the senses.
This nascent bulb lightly smiles,
"We meet again." Gaze pensive.

And in due time, it will outshine itself.
It should come as no surprise.
The child of the Tulip will soon grow,
to be The Mother of the Tulip that will follow.

Through the storms.
Through the rains.
Through the sunshine.
Through the hail.

Young Tulip lives many lives.
Old Tulip dies many deaths.
Somehow,

each day feels anew.
Each night, a jewel.
Each moment is cherished with a grateful breath.

Mother births Child.
Child births Mother.
The rebirth of the Tulip
brings hope yonder.

Preferred Noun

11:57 PM.

Three minutes before midnight
was when they stopped calling him by his name.

Instead, they referred to him as "the body".
The body; how dare they!

Does a flatline determine,
when men, women, and children,

lose their identities,
and become mere nameless bodies?

Does a flatline crown a proper noun,
into a common noun?

Death,

has already taken away so much from us.
Must it take away his name as well?

The White Crayon

Twelve little crayons.
Each, the same height.
Each, a different color.
None feeling forlorn.

Twelve little crayons.
Eager to work on
lighting up someone's life.
Changing someone's world.

One little crayon
feels invisible.
It wants to hold on.
It wants to believe that it is worthy and capable.

One little crayon
watches its friends shrink with age.
Wonders what it did wrong,
as it remains unchanged.

One little crayon
is struggling to hold on.
It cannot understand,
why being white means being invisible in this land.

The White Crayon
in silence, pities its plight.
In anguish, envies its neighbors.
In sadness, dreams of change.

The White Crayon
dreams of a bright future.
It dreams of a future that will be fairer,
to the future White Crayons, in the land of white paper.

The Oil And Water Dance

Armchair experts. Vocal observers.
Debaters. Myth busters. Finger pointers.
Trolls.

So many humans. Such little humanity.
So many triggers. Such little tenacity.
So many voices. Such little virtuosity.

Online. Offline. Full-time. Part-time.
Like Oil and Water, never blending.
Constantly swirling, all day and night.

We Are In This Together

"We are in this together."
Some say it more often than others.
To cleanse their sins,
and console themselves from within.

"We are in this together."
The rich. The poor.
The informed. The ignorant.
The vanquishers. The vanquished.

"We are in this together."
There is no room for prejudice.
There is no room for injustice.
There is no room for malice.

"We are in this together."
Swimming in the remorseless ocean.
Afraid of sinking into the darkness.
Afraid of drowning in our emotions.

"We are in this together."
Fighting for and against each other.
Lovers. Haters. Runners. Screamers.
The lost. The found. The redeemers.

"We are in this together."
Employing one another as driftwood.
Nervously paddling ahead.
Never looking back, ever.

Together,

we choose what to restore.
We choose what to dismember.
We choose whom to forget.
We choose whom to remember.

The Spring Of Saudade

Another vocation. Another relocation.
Perhaps this time it will feel like home.

Another nation. Another station.
Maybe I won't feel as alone.

The more I want these memories to fade,
the more they surface, like a stubborn and crusty stain.

Perhaps they are waiting for me to trade,
my time. My abilities. My name. My sanity.

I cannot wait to selfishly wade
and cut away my strings,

in the Spring of springs,
in The Spring of Saudade.

In Transit

When the lights go out. When the footsteps fade,
and the other voices fall asleep, my inner voice awakes.

Out slide the earrings, the elegant necklace,
the layers of lace, the mascara, the liner,

and the carefully preserved locks of jet-black tresses.
I hear myself chuckling and shying away from the moonlight.

I outline my eyes. I paint my lips.
I adorn myself with stones, metal, and fabric.

Oh, what a sight! Oh, what a feeling!
To be caressed by my untamed imagination, wheeling.

Tomorrow, I will be one step closer.
My bosom will be fuller. My new name will be remembered.

Tomorrow, I will no longer be him.
Tomorrow, I will be her.

The Rescue

She and I,

are more alike than I thought.
Curious eyes. Broken hearts.

Forgiving minds. Arms that reach out.
Eyes that glisten when someone listens.

Always looking for the way back home.
Frequent users of backroads.

Terrible kissers. Even terrible whisperers.
Borderline drifters. Unexplained blisters.

They look at her with admiration,
as she welcomes them without hesitation.

This rescue. This canine. Came into my life,
when I had given up and was reaching for the light.

Truth be told, it is she who rescued me,
and chose to love me unconditionally.

How We Wear Our Shells

To the snail, the shell is its lifeline.
Its anchor. Its sail. Its shelter. Its shrine.

To the hermit crab, no shell is permanent.
Change is imminent. It never settles for drab.

How fascinating that they both need a shell, the accommodating host.
To not feel like a ghost, as they travel from pillar to post.

Us folks. We are no different. We hide our shells. We wear our shells.
We change our shells. We chase other shells.

And what if our shells were to be dismantled?
I wonder,

how many of us would be left unscathed?
How many of us would be left mangled?

The Photographer's Secret

"There's some heavy shadow here."

"Let's try this spot."

"Too many people in the background."

"Tuck your belly in."

"Hold your breath. Don't let it out yet."

"Turn to your left, it's your better side."

"Wait, more people in the background."

"Your smile is too broad. Make it look more authentic."

"Wait, you blinked. Let's try that again."

A photograph. A minute. Frozen in a second.

Did they enjoy the warmth of summertime?

What do you reckon?

The reality is hardly within the smiles,

and certainly not within the frame.

The truth is kept sacred by the photographer.

Always.

I Am Breaking Up With You

New revelations. Same conversations.
New aspirations. Same realizations.

My world revolves around you.
Sometimes it feels like we are now closer.

And then I remember how far apart we really are.
The distance. The silence. The fact that we don't even touch.

I'm tired of watching the others shimmer with mischief,
as they whisper stories and secrets about us.

It's not me. It's you. Are you listening?
Look at me when I'm talking to you.

Earth, I no longer want to be your Moon.
I am breaking up with you.

For real, this time.
For good.

What They Don't Tell You About Loss

What they don't tell you about loss,
is how hard it is to move on.
Getting out of bed was my biggest win today.
Yet, it feels so wrong.

My better part is far from home.
I wasn't prepared to embark on this journey alone.
This house. This room. The window. The view.
Birds and butterflies. Fluttering askew.

How dare they chirp in delight.
How dare the world refuses to stop.
How dare they choose to move on.
Without my life. Without my love.

Life In A Box

The commute to my office now
comprises five steps away from my bed.
The new normal feels more new than normal.
I'll choose a different box today - my kitchen.

We park our cars within little boxes.
We park ourselves by our desks.
Cubicles, cabins, conference rooms.
Cradles and caskets. More boxes.

Working remotely. Virtual realities.
Our children plug themselves into little boxes too.
A box for Science. A box for History.
A box for detention – just to name a few.

"Can you hear me now?"
"Can you see my screen?"
"I think you're on mute."

Great.
More people in little boxes.

Humans on the Moon.
Humans on Mars.

Humans on Earth.

Humans fighting to name the stars.

Our biggest accomplishment thus far?

Building boxes,

that keep raising the bar.

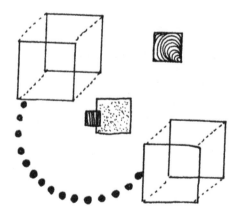

Far From Home

"Where are you from?"

"But where are you *really* from?"

"Where are your parents from?"

"Your accent is perfect."

"What is your birth name?"

"You sound like you grew up here."

"You sound like one of us."

"Can I touch your hair?"

"The color of your skin is unique."

"Meet the diversity hire."

I hear these words, and some more.

It's a rude awakening when I'm reminded once again.

How far away I truly am from home.

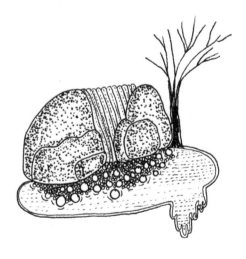

19

Happiness And Success

What a foolish thing to ask,
"Would you rather…
… be happy or successful?"
As if the two were in separate flasks.

As if one were monumental.
And the other not as eventful.
As if one were more desirable.
And the other, less fashionable.

What if I am happily successful?
What if I am successfully happy?
What if I do carry regrets?
What makes you think that I would trade,

my failures? My flaws? My shortcomings?
My losses? My tumbles? My crashes?
My bruises? My scars?

Yes, I am exactly where I need to be.
Yes, I am exactly who I want to be.
Yes, I would do it all over again.
Yes, I drew my strength, from my pain.

Greetings

I smile at the mirror
and my reflection smiles back at me.
Perhaps the teeth ought to be more contained.
Is that acne I see?

I smile again.
Teeth more contained.
This is as good as it gets.
The blemishes are far from restrained.

Meeting new people.
Learning new names.
Trying to sound appealing, not feeble.
Trying to appear interesting, not insane.

A firm handshake?
A well-intentioned hug?
Is this my big break?
Please, fate. Don't pull the rug.

"Hey, how's it going?"
"Hello."
"Hi."
"Pleased to meet you."

I promise to greet you,

just as I mean it

if you promise to greet me,

just as you mean it too.

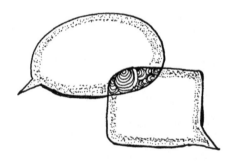

Quiet Spaces

Between the predicament, and the solution.
Between the persecution, and the consolation.
Between the resolution, and the revolution.
Between the creation, and the destruction.

There is a quiet space.
A spark's birthplace.
Where the gears turn,
and the coals of desire burn.

Before the thought kindles the heart.
Before the heart ignites the mind.
Before the hand begins to craft.
Before the lips speak unresigned.

There is a quiet space
where the inner voice resides
before it steps out and begins to interlace,
with the voices outside.

Time Is A Construct

Once given, impossible to reclaim.
Once lost, impossible to replace.

Time is an enigma. So accurate yet so vague.
Time is a construct. Spinning numerous tales.

Some follow the moon. Some follow the stars.
Some follow the sun. Some are at war,

to decide how many hours make a day.
How many days make a week.

How many weeks make a month.
How many months make a year.

Time watches. The ever-observant bystander.
Time smirks as it holds back its candor.

Time is a construct - an illusion.
To both the fools and the wise, struggling to reach a conclusion.

Culinary Chemistry

Cumin. Cardamom.
Crispy poppadom.
Steaming rice. Supple lentils.
Feasting like the Emperor of Rome.
So much power
within a humble meal.
Sugar. Salt. Flour.
Paprika. Cornmeal.

Culinary chemistry.

The ingredients churn playfully.
First bite. First love.
Last bite. Eyes look above,
in delight, in gratitude.
Some ingredients are known.
Some ingredients are new.

When the weary travelers chew,
they long to belong and taste something,
that tastes true.

Shine Your Light

Before, they barely noticed me at the table.

Now, they rise as I enter the room.

Before, they barely remembered my name.

Now, they salute me by my surname.

Before, I was a nobody.

Now, I attract everybody.

What changed?

Me.

I brought my chair to the table.

I spoke up.

I chose to be the advocate,

for a fair chance. For an overdue change.

I lifted others around me.

The voiceless. The powerless.

The ones who were growing tired and restless.

True power,

is not with the one who outshines.

But with the one who shines their light,
on the embers hiding in the shadows.
On the voices muffled by the echoes.

True power seems invisible.
But it's felt by everyone,
everywhere.

What Makes Us Human

How ironic.
The passion with which they talk about happiness,
is different from their understanding of unhappiness.

In pursuit of contentment.
In pursuit of gratification.
In pursuit of satisfaction.

Does that mean,
that we do not learn in sadness?
That we do not learn in disappointment?

Is the state of relaxation,
the art of meditation,
the craft of contemplation,

an excision of hurt?
An erasure of shame?
A deletion of depression?

An extraction, of what makes us human?

Learning How To Fear

"Don't touch that."
"Don't eat that."
"Don't wear that."
"Don't talk back."
"Don't waste your time."
"Don't play in the dirt."
"Don't play with them."
"Don't marry her."
"Don't come back."
"Don't be like him."

We learn how to love,
with shrewdness.
We learn how to fear,
with crudeness.

Heroes And Villains

There are those who are willing
to sacrifice their love,
to save the world.

And then there are those who are willing
to sacrifice their world,
to save their love.

Heroes.
Villains.
They walk among us.

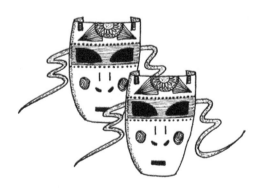

Part 2 – The Guide

The Queen Of The Night

A blossom. A year.
She draws travelers from far and near.
Her fragrance lets you know that you are home.

So, stay for a while.
Let her perfume wrap you in this cold.
Under this starry moonlight.

Here today. Gone tomorrow.
But memories of her will linger,
until the next time you meet her.

She truly is a sight for sore eyes.
Meet your guide,
The Queen of the Night.

Blood And Water

Blood by default demands faith and devotion.
Blood is believed to be a reliable vault.

Blood is where loyalties are kept sacred.
Blood is where traditions are followed unquestioned.

Blood is why sacrifices are helplessly profound.
Blood is why compromises are weighed and graded.

But what of water?
The life-giver. The liquid sustainer. The coveted quencher.

Does it have no needs? No wants? No demands?
Blood by default is arrogantly thicker than water.

Alas,

it is blood that clots.
It is blood that falters.

The Art Of Losing

This mansion of your invention,

has left you floating in suspension.

You lay there hoping that tomorrow will be the day,

when someone will remember your name,

and hold you gently because they care.

But mostly because they want to be there,

to chase away the demons that plague you.

To displace the memories that taunt you.

To help create moments, that will leave you smiling.

But no, you have it all and more.

And yet, you are paddling with no oars.

No one to call you. No one to hold you.

No one to pacify you.

No one to stand beside you,

as you waste away in your gilded gloom.

A Broken Compass

What makes a compass trustworthy
is not its engraving, but its ability,
to magnetically align itself with the Earth.

The same can be said about our purpose.
It takes an alignment of two elements.

If the heart does not accept what the hand does,
then the head will continue to spin aimlessly,

like a broken compass.

Half-Baked Intentions

Here they come again.
Trucks of food, water, clothing, and relief.
Carefully weighed and allocated.

There are three sides to every war.

The faction on one side. The faction on the other,
and the faction that declares,
to help the ones caught in despair.

Peace talks. Tradeoffs. A photo-op. A campaign.
A revolution, born from the ashes of good intentions.
An assault on our right to just live without pain.

Here they come again. In their polished covers,
as we remain broken and blood-stained.
To tell us that help is on the way.
To convince us that tomorrow will be a better day.

Here they come again,
with the fruits of their circumventions.
With their debatable commissions.
With their pitiful, half-baked intentions.

Hand-Written Destiny

Head Line.
Heart Line.
Sun Line.
Fate Line.
Life Line.

So many lines,
etched on our palms.

The puzzled palm reader is struggling to tell
how this person without both arms,

has discovered heaven,
and survived hell.

Suitable Questions

"Did you kiss back?"
"What time did you get home?"
"Were you alone?"
"Why did you not call someone?"
"How long have you known?"
"What did you do right after?"
"Why did you not get out sooner?"

No victim would ever
describe these questions as suitable.

And yet, these victims show up
to answer them.

So that another victim,
may be spared.

The Couple In The Photograph

Another wedding story.
Another album with highlight reels.

Friends and family,
reliving the glorious moments of the couple in the photograph.

I hope the day will come
when the same people, the ones I love,

will relive the glorious memories,
of two women becoming one.

I want that for us. I want us to be
that couple in the photograph.

Accepted.
Loved.
Freed.

Unspoken Words

That glance. That nod.
That crinkle of the eye.

When we meet, and we greet,
without exchanging names.

Day in. Day out.
We, strangers, become more familiar.

We say so much,
without saying a word.

Theft By Denial

The loss of life,
is the greatest loss of all.

Who are you to judge
whether this loss is worthy or not,

of being acknowledged,
of being assigned,

a resting place that feels familiar,
a gathering space for the familial?

You claim they selfishly took their own lives.
You gift them unmarked graves to quieten the noise.

If only you knew, how they kept screaming for help.
If only you knew, what it means to scream in silence.

Taming Hate

Hate, I'm told, is a strong word.

It's what happens when dislike swells unapologetically.

It's what happens when intent gets bruised by impact.

Hate takes many forms, as a noun and a verb.

I wonder if Hate has a fear. I wonder if Hate feels lonely.

I wonder if Hate can lie convincingly.

I've seen how Hate steals when it's masked by passion.

I've seen how Hate obliterates by being the champion of destruction.

Hate, I'm told, is the opposite of Love.

The two cannot co-exist within a conflicted heart.

Hate, I'm told, must be tamed

before it engulfs you and changes your name.

From The Bottom Of My Glass

At the bottom of my glass is an unruly ending.
A truth I'm afraid to speak. Tears that I'm holding back.

Unlike my heart which is at its fullest at the bottom.
The more this tonic fills my glass, the heavier my heart seems to feel.

Perhaps it will be forgotten in the morn.
Just one more. This glass feels lighter now.

I'm not ready for the bottom of this glass.
Not yet. Please, just one more.

A Word So Versatile

"Sorry."
Translation: I apologize.

"Sorry."
Translation: I apologize for nothing.

"Sorry."
Translation: You must be hurting.

"Sorry."
Translation: Go back.

"Sorry."
Translation: It's not my fault, but it will soothe you.

Sorry.

A word with many feelings.
A word with many meanings.
A word versatile enough,
to be both a truth and a lie.

A Good Teacher

Have you met a good teacher?
Someone who teaches
others to teach?

Someone who speaks what the learners speak?
Someone who makes you feel,
smarter than you did after you entered the room?

The strength of knowledge
is not harnessed by accumulating it,
and feeding it to the worthy.

A good teacher is approachable.
A good teacher is one,
who is teachable.

The Grounded Bird

Not every nest is designed to be a safe place for the eggs.
Not every bird is destined to fly at will.
Some birds are felled when they are fast asleep.
Gently shoved. Rolled. Pushed over the edge.

Soft thud. A bird survives. Somehow. It's not dead yet.
This bird, once nested. Sadly, now grounded.
It was destined to soar up.
Instead, it crashed down. Confounded.

Poor birdie must now carry its broken wings.
It must quickly learn that it is no longer safe to sing.
It has to now survive this new world,
where the smoke and clouds, collide and curl.

Poor birdie.
What good are your wings now?
Poor birdie.
You grounded bird.

Asking For A Friend

Will they think less of me,
if I say no?

Will they think I'm weak,
if I cry?

Will they leave me behind,
if I bleed?

Will they forget my name,
if I refuse to look the other way?

In a world that is authentically fake,
how can I be the genuine me?

Any tips and tricks?
I'm asking for a friend.

One Vision

Isn't it incredible how the left eye and the right eye
both see the same thing,
but can't see each other,
without a mirror?

Isn't it incredible how if one eye gets hurt
it hurts the other eye too
and looking into the mirror,
feels scarier?

Behind That Hill

A new opportunity. A new friend.
Awaited her behind that hill.
She would wake up and wonder,
what she might discover, behind that hill.

Anytime she gave directions she would explain,
"Take a turn, around that hill,"
and she would wonder why the others,
would glance and grin every time she mentioned the hill.

This is her blessing
and her curse.
To be as close to the hill,
as the hill is close to her.

She lives
in blissful oblivion.
She is the ever optimistic
rhinoceros.

A Blind Date

No one dates like a bat does.
Blind. In the dark.
So many unknowns, but

sharp ears. Listening ears.
Ears that can tell,

when you're far.
When you're here.
When you're lost
in your thoughts, and your fears.

Such a pity that we cannot
rely on our eyes
to filter the truth,
and the lies.

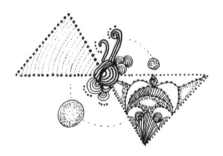

A Conversion Of Sorts

His beliefs opposed hers.
Her beliefs opposed his.
Both argued and debated. Both had a reason to show,

why their side, was the *right-er* side.
Why their beliefs, were the way of life.
Eyes would lock, and so would their opinions.

A battle of words. A battle of convictions.
Each on a mission to convert the other.
And in the end,

they married each other instead.

Saying Yes To Saying No

Knowing when to say,
"No"
will empower you.

Knowing when to say,
"No more"
will liberate you.

But You Seem Fine

"But you seem fine."

The words that you're cursed to hear
when you're hurting, without it showing.

If only they knew,
not every wound bleeds.

Love Is Not Blind

We've had it wrong
this whole time.

Love is not blind.

It simply chooses to look away.

Part 3 – The Pilgrim

The Faithful Sunflower

Oh, faithful sunflower.

You shine with your magnificence
as you blindly follow the sun at every turn,
with an unchallenged devotion that yearns.

Tell me, oh loyal sunflower.

Does your faith waver with each passing hour?
What if your god, your sun, were to touch you one day?
Would you bloom in delight, or burn in dismay?

Morning Rituals

First light. The eyes open unwillingly.
Reaching for the phone. What day is it?
There is somewhere I have to be.
On-time, this time.

When did I become a slave to my routine?
Hot water. Cold water. Waking me up, from head to toe.
Hot coffee. Cold weather. What is today's date? Why is it so cold?

It should have been different today.
There must be a new ritual with a new name.
Tomorrow will be different. Tomorrow is another day.

Tomorrow, I promise.
This ritual won't get its way.
Tomorrow, most certainly,
this ritual won't be the same.

A Secret Between The Gods

"How many gods do you pray to?"

"At least twenty-three."

"How lucky."

"Why? How many do you pray to?"

"Just one."

"Don't worry…

… I'll put in a good word for you with my army of gods."

"Thanks, but don't tell my God."

"My gods! Is your god jealous?"

"Very. Has a bad temper too."

Divine Imagination

Painted hills. Rugged mountains. Diverse trees.
Shades of blue, brown, gray, and green.
Tufted skies. Feathery horizons.
The oceans and the heavens interweave.

Living beings, all shapes, and sizes.
Inanimate entities, full of surprises.
Each and everything,
a pigment, a fragment of the divine imagination.

God is an artist.
We are a part of the evolving creation.
This Masterpiece is far from completion.
And it should come as no surprise.

Red fights Blue.
White fights Black.
Brown fights Yellow.

Colors in chaos.
No friends.
Only opponents.

I feel sorry for God

for choosing to work with a canvas,

that is constantly conflicted,

and is hiding behind the rampaging colors.

Mama, The Wise

"Mama, what is my purpose? …
What is my true calling? …
How do I know if I'm on the right path?"

She held my face with her gnarled, yet steady hands.
She looked into my eyes with confidence,
as she said,

"My love. My little one …
Your purpose is not singular…
In this lifetime, may you live a hundred lives."

Creatures Of Symbols

Carved in wood. Engraved in stone.
Inscriptions that are understood. Relics that remain unknown.

Times may have changed, but our habits have not.
Artifacts are exchanged, as the tapestry gets riddled with knots.

Meanings assigned, based on a sign,
that our ancestors witnessed eons ago.

Different interpretations. Lost translations.
The Wise can't tell a raven from a crow.

Does the sword mean war? Does the sword mean strength?
Whose arm do you use, to measure arm's length?

Was the fruit forbidden, or simply forgotten?
And was it delighted to be held by the hand of a virgin?

Persons, people, peoples.
We are creatures, who live and die for our symbols.

Embracing Grace

When your burden feels heavy. When your feet seem unsteady.
Give yourself grace.
You will progress, at your own pace.

When the questions outweigh the answers. When doubt lingers longer.
Give yourself grace.
Your efforts are not misplaced.

When the newness overwhelms you. When nostalgia revisits you.
Give yourself grace.
Everything has a purpose, a time, and a place.

When all is lost. When it feels like there is little to live for.
Give yourself grace.
Someone is longing to feel your embrace.

A Good Bargain

It takes two to strike a good bargain.
To haggle and negotiate, again, and again.

If one hand must not know the good deeds done by the other,
then should I be more discrete about my offerings at the altar?

Chants. Hymns. Songs of praise. I haggle and negotiate,
again, and again.

Father Almighty. Heavenly Mother. Divine Child.
Prophets. Disciples. Saints. Angels.

Have my sacrifices been reconciled?
What does your ledger say? Does it go by first name or last name?

I will not lose heart. I will not lose faith.
I will haggle and negotiate, again, and again.

The Empty Chair

Lights. Music. Festivities.
Ornaments stud the halls and the trees.
The same song and dance every once a year.

Families united. Memories rekindled. Boxes of cheer.
We feast. We embrace. We exchange gifts.
I wonder if I've had too much wine. This is probably my fifth.

No matter how hard I try. I can't seem to avoid
this feeling that I don't belong here.
I'm mostly tongue-tied.

At the dining table, hands exchange dishes
along with crafted smiles, and empty wishes.
Paired with full plates.

I wonder if they can tell. I wonder if they care,
to notice that even though I'm at the table,
I'm one with the empty chair.

In Another Life

Two lovers meet for one last time.
A moment so bittersweet, it almost feels like a crime.
Born into different creeds.
Different faiths. Different beliefs.

Theirs was a union that would not be blessed.
No jubilations. No acknowledgments.
Only grief.
Only unrest.

"If we were taught to love, then why is our love wrong?"
"Because ours is the kind of love that doesn't belong."
"If love conquers all then why won't we win?"
"Because to them, our love is a sin."

"Does this mean that we can never be together?"

"Perhaps we can. Perhaps we will.
Perhaps we will be able to love each other.
Fearlessly. Unregretfully.
In another life."

Chasing Tomorrow

"I promise I will work harder tomorrow."
"Tomorrow is a new opportunity."
"I will start over tomorrow."
"Tomorrow things will be better."
"Let's work on this tomorrow."
"Worry not, there is always tomorrow."
"At least we still have tomorrow."
"I will see you tomorrow."

We blindly chase tomorrow,
as swiftly as we can.
Placing bets on the future.
Forever altering our plans.

But what good is tomorrow,
when it finally retires?
When Death chooses to visit us today,
and we have no tomorrow left for hire?

A Temple With No Walls

Imagine a temple with no walls.
No portraits. No idols. No halls.

Imagine a temple with no doors.
No windows. No stained glass. No floors.

Imagine a temple so open.
So broad. So wide. So high.

Imagine a temple that is always forgiving.
No questions asked. Always welcoming.

"Where is this temple?", you ask?

Are you ready?
Close your eyes.

Long-Distance Call

I've been calling You by the same name
for as long as I can remember.

I've been reading the passages passed down to me.
I've been following the traditions prescribed by my ancestors.

Perhaps today is the day that You will finally hear me.
Rumor has it, that You go by many names.

Some are afraid, to imagine what You might look like.
Are You more dreamlike? Or ghostlike?

"Keep the faith.", they said. "Your faith will save you."
Is my faith a banner for The Living or The Dead?

When I pray more often, does my voice get louder?
When I pray less often, does Your love for me turn sour?

In The Name Of Contrition

Fasting on Tuesdays.

Wearing The Sacred Thread on Wednesdays.

Abstinence on Thursdays.

No meat on Fridays.

Charitable acts on Saturdays.

A visit to The Sacred Place on Sundays.

Mondays we reflect and prepare,

for our acts of contrition.

For our assured admission

to the promised Paradise,

where love flows freely,

without a price.

The Prophet Among Us

The arrival. The reckoning.
Lost flocks wait anxiously for their shepherd.

A ray of light. The beckoning.
Blind sheep follow the leopard.

Nirvana. Bliss. Utopia. The path ahead is mighty confusing.
The visions. The tongues. The inscriptions. Uncontrolled diplopia.

They inspire their followers to move mountains.
They perform acts of wonders. They leave the masses wanting more.

They call themselves The Prophets.
On a crusade to guide us, The Lost Misfits.

I've heard of a prophet that goes by no name.
I've heard of a prophet that is a parent to every orphan.

I've heard of a prophet that listens, to lighten one's burden.
Said prophet is someone powerful, yet ordinary.

Said prophet walks among us, performing tiny miracles,
in a world that is overwhelmingly scary.

Behold These Beads

Behold these beads.
Your solace when in need.

Smooth to the touch,
but worn out from being the crutch,

to your desires, to your devotion.
To set your plans in motion.

Quivering lips. Closed eyes. Behold these beads.
Your custodian, from sunset to sunrise.

The Making Of A Prayer

"Papa, what is a prayer?"
"It's a request to our Creator, our ultimate Provider."

"What should I pray for, Papa?"
"Anything you want. Anything you desire."

"Will my prayer make Mama come back?"
"Mama can't come back, love. She is resting in Paradise."

"Is Mama happy there?"
"Yes, she is. She is with our Creator now."

"Can I pray to see her?"
"Darling, she sees you, and will always watch over you."

"Will our Creator mind if I pray to Mama instead?"

A Religion Called Love

We celebrate, in love.

We mourn, in love.

We are whole, in love.

We are broken, in love.

We are believers, in love.

We are fools, in love.

We hurt, in love.

We heal, in love.

We fight, in love.

We die, in love.

We sing, in love.

We love, in love.

Above all,

Love.

Demons In Daylight

I have many things that I want to say.
My thoughts taunt me. They know that I'm prey,

to the Louder Ones, the Bigger Ones,
the Sharper Ones, the Smarter Ones,

the Gilded Ones, the Respected Ones,
the Ones who swing wildly, between *aye* and *nay*.

The demons we hear of are not the Wandering Undead.
They walk like us. They talk like us.

They look like us. They think like us.
They do not wait for the clock to strike midnight.

They have no reason to hide,
as they dance around us, in daylight.

Vilomah

I've stopped asking, "Why me?"
I've been praying, "Please, not anyone else."
Tubes. Tapes. Wires. As far as the eye can see.
Lungs feeling tighter with every breath.

When death marks a family member,
a husband becomes a widower,
a wife - a widow, a child - an orphan,
but a parent?

A loss without a name is a heavier burden.

What will they call my parents, after I'm gone?
Will time be kind? Will they move on?
Will they be repeating the same stories
hoping to rekindle my spirit?

"Sorry for your loss." "My heartfelt condolences."
What else can be said under these circumstances?

Mama, Papa, I'm afraid.
This pain won't go away.
Mama, Papa, I'm sorry.
I wish I could stay.

This is *Vilomah.*
This feels unfair,
unjust.

Death is a hoarder,
of lives lived and unborn.
Such a ruthless warder.

Mama, Papa, please don't cry.
Though my heart will stop beating soon,
remember that I will love you for life.

Take My Hand

"How long have you been standing there?"

"Not that long."

"You look nothing like I imagined."

"I know. I get that all the time."

"Time… is it time then?"

"I believe so."

"It's too soon. I'm not ready."

"No one ever is, really."

"Is this going to hurt?"

"Not at all."

"I don't want to be alone."

"You're not. Take my hand."

"But they said we all die alone."

"Well, they were wrong."

Part 4 – The Pioneer

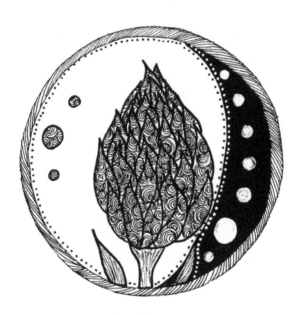

The Rise Of The Protea

In the face of adversity, there is strength in diversity.
In the face of uncertainty, there is strength in contingency.

Pioneers are not born as pioneers. They are fashioned from the ruins,
of failures, of endeavors, of unanswered prayers.

The Pioneer. The Protea.
How similar they are.

Beacons of self-transformation.
No second thoughts. No hesitations.

Taking chances. More than once.
Not a slave to tradition.

Rhythms And Rhymes

There is a rhythm to everything that we do.
The way our hearts beats. The way our pots brew.

Laughing. Crying. Walking out in anger.
A rhythm for friends. A rhythm for strangers.

Some rhythms are learned. Some rhythms are earned.
Some rhythms are disowned. Some rhythms are loaned.

We are the sum of our rhythms. We are the products of our rhymes.
We are the makers of our tempos. We are the singers of lost times.

Mother Failure

Every action. Every turn.
Nests a lesson, waiting to be learned.

The masters. The experts.
All connoisseurs of failures.

Before the title of being skillful,
and being worthy examples

were bestowed upon them
they learned that,

failure is not a force to be averted.
Failure is the womb of Success.

The Art Of Giving

"Give it your all."
What does that mean?

Perhaps my all is your some?
Or maybe your some is my none?

The White Jasmine Tree blooms freely.
Flowers and fragrance. Giving is a part of its elegance.

The clouds flock together to gift us the weather.
Rain. Hail. Snow. Thunder. Different textures. Different colors.

It's ironic how people, the masterminds of taking,
the questioners of freely sharing,

have so many misgivings,
about the art of giving.

Clouds And Silver Lies

"My sister passed away."
"Be strong."

"My husband may not make it."
"Be strong."

"I was assaulted."
"Be strong."

"It's not working out."
"Be strong."

"I have nothing to live for."
"Be strong."

Be strong.

Two words they tell you
to embellish your dark cloud with silver.

The see-through kind. The kind that makes you,
feel lonely in a crowd.

An Educated Guess

Knowledge is power, or so they said.
Cum laude. Magna. Summa.
Embossed. Preserved in frames.
Behind sheets of glass, they rest.

How many initials does it take,
to make one well educated?
How many mouths must go hungry?
For the educated to join the elite of the accepted?

Is there nothing to learn from the uneducated?
Then why be so stern with the ones who live closer to reality,
with the ones who make better-educated guesses,

with the ones who are differently educated,
than the distant, decorated, and isolated faculty?

The Leader Leading Others

A movement is a result
of a singular becoming plural.

It starts with an idea of an individual.
Slightly scared. Slightly intimidated.

Until a spark lights up in them,
to pass the torch to someone else.

To inspire more individuals, to lead others.
Thus, a movement is a journey

of one leader,
leading others.

Lasting Legacy

The Strongest. The Biggest. The Fastest.
They race to create unforgettable creases in time.

They compete to be remembered by the people waiting in line,
to shine, just like they did.

The Strongest. The Biggest. The Fastest.
They are recorded and recalled by the ones who ardently follow them.

By the ones who got left behind.
By *The Lastest.*

Fortune Favors The Crazy

Someone thought it would be clever,

to drink off another mammal's udder.
To roast bright berries.
To touch electricity.
To smoke a leaf.
To poke a vein.
To be touched by a venom's toxicity.
To formulate an edible ecstasy.

An idea that sounds brilliant today,
was foolish, insane, and absurd yesterday.

We have made it this far you see,
because someone was bold enough,
to be crazy.

Starting Now

"Mama,
my teacher asked me
what I want to be when I grow up."

"My darling,
you can be anyone you want to be,
starting now."

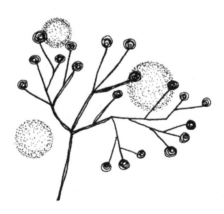

In Uniforms We Trust

The banners we wear.
The anthems we boldly declare.

The stripes we earn. The honors we relentlessly share.
What does it mean to be in uniform?

Does it reassure loyalty? Does it embody trust?
Does it flaunt piety? Does it secretly lust?

For power?
For respect?

For towers to be erected,
amid the ashes and the wreckage?

Do you trust the uniform that you wear?
Does said uniform trust its people everywhere?

Perhaps there might come a day
when you will wake up and realize,

your uniform feels no pride.
Your uniform was born mute, deaf, and blind.

Fear The Weak

The feeble. The pale. The meek.
The hungry. The tired. The weak.

Knuckled down to circumstances.
Never blessed with fair chances.

The Losers. The Quitters. The Hopeless.
They go by many names.

Do not be fooled by the voiceless.
Silence can tear down many gates.

Fear the ones who have lost it all,
for there is nothing more to lose.

Fear the ones with nothing to their name.
The Nobodies gather and infuse.

Fear the ones who appear weak,
for their strength is about to peak.

Dear Misguided Misanthrope

I admire your passion.
Your fury. Your questioning questions.
The rickety stage upon which you stand.

So bold. So brave. So devoted to what you have to say.
Do not be fooled by the rattle you hear.
The sound of empty vessels may soothe your ears.

Did it burn when you learned that I'm not in the cage?
Did it hurt when you cut yourself,
because of your bottomless rage?

You clipped my wings
while forgetting that I could still walk.
You silenced my tongue
while forgetting that my voice was still loud.

Dear Misguided Misanthrope,
here's sending you thoughts, prayers, and a truckload of hope.
The path you're on is a slippery slope.

No Time To Rest

Some cycles, on time.
Some cycles, far behind.
Bleeding between the legs.

"Why so serious?"
"Smile."
"Man up.",
they said.

She extends lineages. She extends her name.
They say she was born wild.
They insist on her being tamed.

Not enough fabric. Not enough bandages.
To cover her scars,
the trophies from her battles and wars.

Some cycles, on time.
Some cycles, far behind.
Breasts painfully tender.

No, not now.
She will not surrender.
Clocks ticking. Wombs shrinking.

Passing test after test.
Preparing for the next.
Dabbing worn eyes.
Looking her best.

Juggling her personas.
Juggling others' lives.
Always showing up.
Refusing to hide.

Her name is Woman.
She fights for herself, and the rest.
Her name is Woman.
So much to do. No time to rest.

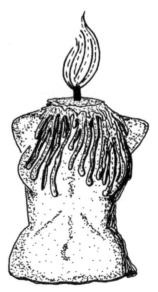

The Innocent Thorn

Without me she is nothing.
And yet,
they sing songs in her name.

Rose always catches their eyes.
She captivates them
as she leaves them mesmerized.

How unfortunate for me
for they don't see,
I serve one purpose, and one purpose only.

To help Rose grow.
Taller. Stronger.
More beautiful.

She claws her way over the other
unsuspecting flowers - her lovers.
She steals their thrones.

She steals their light.
She climbs freely because of me.
Her trusting Thorn.

I am the silent witness,

to her being someone else's mistress.

I am also the one who defends her

from the prying hands that try to pluck her.

All that I am is her innocent Thorn.

But all that I get,

are scowls and scorns.

The Sound Of Life

These vibrations.
These movements.
Are the sounds I feel
in silence.

I speak with my hands.
I speak with my eyes.
I wonder if you realize how I long to hear,
your laughter.

The way you squeal.
The waves crashing against the shore.
The sound you make when you enjoy your meal.
The way you chuckle when we're watching a movie.

The leaves of the trees rustle,
like an audience giving a round of applause.
The sound of the mundane.
The crowd. The traffic. The wind. The bustle.

People lost in conversation about their hustles.
The sound of victory.
The sound of defeat.
The sound of your voice, soothing me to sleep.

I wish my ears could hear again.
Even for a moment.
Just once more.

I miss the sounds of everyday life.
I miss the sounds that get louder
every time I close my eyes.

Own Your Name

First name.

Last name.

Middle name.

Family name.

Surname.

Maiden name.

Former name.

Different names.

Same person.

Names are not tied to faces.

Names are tied to feelings.

Be the unforgettable name.

Be the name that is healing.

Lead By Example

To the unknowns.

To the ones feeling like imposters.

To the ones without a title.

Do not wait for the perfect moment.

Do not wait for the perfect time.

Do not wait for the perfect follower.

Lead.

Lead blindly.

Lead by example.

Still

Is it their age that surprises you
or the fact that they can still walk?
Without the walker, without the crutch
of expectations outlined by you?

Is it their age that surprises you
or the fact that they can still talk?
As if it happened yesterday.
So articulate. Never ceasing to captivate.

Is it their age that surprises you
or the fact that they can still swim?
Cover laps. Strides like butterflies.
Simply float on a whim.

Is it their age that surprises you
or the fact that they are still aware?
Very there.
Splitting your doubts with their will.

Why must you fear aging and chase the elusive youth?
When the aged still open their welcoming arms and stand by you?

Unchartered Waters

Unchartered waters
do not stop
a sailor
from sailing.

Pray tell,
what is stopping you
from trying something new,
today?

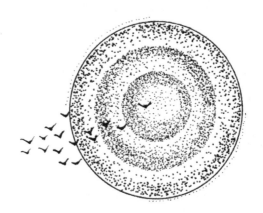

To Fight For A Stranger

Are you willing to fight for someone
whose name you can't pronounce?

Are you willing to face the den of danger
for a stranger who once gave you their blood?

How do you know which side is the right side?
When the cries of people fleeing and dying,

have been displaced
by the chants of the Messengers of Lies?

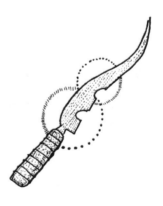

Malleable Metal

I once searched far and wide. North and South. East and West,
for someone to call my role model
to help me become a better version of myself.

After hitting several dead ends I have now taken it upon myself,
to be born again. To metamorphize.
To die a different death.

It takes fire to purify gold.
And I am the malleable metal.
Beaten. Torched. Embossed. Fettled.

Feel my luster defiantly unfold,
as I brazenly engrave
my stories untold.

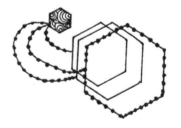

Part 5 – The Settler

The Elements And The Lotus

Earth. Water. Fire. Air.
These elements prance everywhere.
For the lotus that takes quick notice,
home is where these elements flare.

The roots bury deep. The blossoms and the leaves,
reach for the sun and the air. The water adopts not just the lotus,
but also, the critters that come along with it.
The elements and The Lotus.

They glorify each other.
Thus, being at home and being the home,
to the ones who are resting,
and to the ones who roam.

Love Is Fluid

Crisp linen. Freshly made bed.

Thriving houseplants.

Coffee. Mug of my own.

Fur babies. Human babies.

Lemonade on a hot summer's day.

A shoulder to fall asleep on while watching TV.

The person you turn to when you're laughing hysterically.

Chai. Homemade.

Walking barefoot on the grass.

Children being children.

Open spaces.

A heartfelt apology.

That phone call from an old friend.

Holding hands in silence.

Birthday cake. Breakfast in bed.

Feeling seen. Feeling heard. Feeling loved.

Loving back, undeterred. Loving, just because.

Love is fluid.

It flows in many directions.

Love is fluid.

It keeps flowing despite one's objections.

The Weight Of Happiness

"Mama, do you have to work today?"

"Yes, honey. We need the money."

"Papa, will you play with me?"

"Sorry, love. I have to work."

"Because we need the money?"

"Yes, because we need the money."

"How much money, Papa?"

"You can't count that high yet."

"What if I climb the chair? Can I count higher then?"

"Oh, Sweet Pea. You sure can make an old man laugh."

"Why do we need the money, Papa?"

"So that we can be happy."

"Would seven boxes of money be enough?"

"Yes, it should."

"Happiness sounds heavy, Papa."

The Landlings

Pastures like beaten brass.
Clouds form a drifting carcass.
New lands. New horizons.
For the future. For the children.

Tribes against tribes.
Borders redefined.
More hungry humans
claiming the Earth as theirs.

Perpetually feeding their growing girths.
Perpetually quenching their unquenchable thirsts.
These mortals. These *Landlings*.
Living like immortal beings.

They live in obscurity.
They form councils and committees.
Earth is not theirs for the taking.
It is these *Landlings* who will be taken.

As they sink. As they get engulfed by the earth,
and slowly decompose into what they're truly worth.

Earth, their Mother,
watches in silence.
Mourns in silence.
Waits in silence.

To annihilate,
Her blessing
and Her curse,
the *Landlings*.

A World Between Two Worlds

Oh, little one.
How you breathe at ease.
What are your dreams made of?
Would you gurgle one more time for me, please?

Oh, little one.
My universe.
So many adventures await you.
So many experiences are waiting to be discovered.

Between these stories. Between these legacies.
Are a mother and a father wondering,
how to raise you in a world so conflicted?
There was a time when his kind and my kind,

were forbidden from loving each other.
From wanting the same things.
From believing in, and fighting for
the same wins.

Oh, little one. Rest assured.
We will create a world of our own
from the stitches that bind,
these two bleeding worlds.

Just Breathe

Another night of doubt and anxiety.
What if I won't wake up tomorrow?
What if I can't reach my phone?
What if my inhaler runs out?

"Just breathe."
But how hard can I breathe?
Yesterday I could climb the stairs.
Today, I cannot.

"Just breathe."
I'm not dead on the outside.
Yet I'm slowly dying on the inside.
I'm terrified of the person I see in the mirror.

"Just breathe."
I hear the phantom ventilator again.
What day is it today? Whose birthday am I forgetting?
The brain fog is slowly erasing my memories.

"Just breathe."

The Translator's Burden

We may speak the same tongue,
and still, hear what is being said differently.

Enunciation.
Inflection.
Tonality.

What gets lost in translation
are not words,
but feelings.

What gets lost in translation
are not connotations,
but stories.

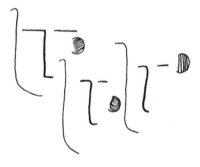

Lessons From Lily

"Mama, what do the trees dream about?"
"Mama, why do grown-ups use words that I cannot?"
"Mama, why must I hug someone when I don't want to?"
"Mama, must I get along with the others, even when they hurt me?"
"Mama, does your ring mean that only Daddy can love you?"

Lily.
Aged 5.

Curious.
Clever.
Compassionate.

My daughter's questions
are life's reminders
that I still have lessons,

to learn.
To unlearn.
And to remember.

Resting Place

Not many draw a life circle,
like the salmon does.

As its time draws near, it swims across
the bodies of water that feel familiar.

It's almost poetic.
How the salmon lays itself to rest.

New paths paved for its children.
The same path braved for its deathbed.

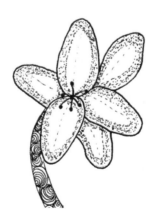

Just A Man In The Park

The stares. The glares.
Interrupting this beautiful day.

This bench was empty. The weather was inviting.
The coveted sunshine told me it was okay,

to sit here and just be alone with my thoughts.
To feel alive. To forget. To numb the pain.

I promise.
I'm not a creep.

Please let me be.
I promise.

I'm just a man in the park,
enjoying the sunshine and the forgiving breeze.

RSVP Is Not Required

Sometimes, as a guest.
Sometimes, as a host.
Sometimes it shows up
uninvited, unconcerned,
with you, and yours.

It may leave
with or without your permission.
With or without a fleeting glance.
With or without a promise,
to come back.

This is Love.
RSVP is not required.

Mortgaged Hands

The ideal lifestyle for you,
may not be worthwhile to me.

Somehow between the compromises.
The sacrifices. The negotiations.

I agreed.
To settle. To trim away little by little,

at our painted reality.
I agreed to say "Yes." What I meant was "No."

Is this how we're supposed to grow?
Here lies the deed to this land.

At the price of my
mortgaged hands.

Loud Silences

It's not easy for me to admit,

that I know.
And that I have always known.
But chose to remain silent.

Wishing for it to go away,
instead of building an asylum.
It's not easy for me to admit,

that my name has been displaced by another.
That another person shares meaningful laughs with you.
That you wished someone else was standing here, in my stead.

How do I break this silence between us?

How do I stop
this deafening silence,
from getting louder?

The Mango And The Mango Tree

I was born on this soil.
These were the skies that comforted me.
My kin. My clan. My tribe.

They witnessed
the same sunlight.
The same moonlight.
The same stars that shimmered in the sky.

Can you blame a mango for not tasting like an apple?
Can you blame the mango for being sour?

Why can't you comprehend how my sweet nectar flows?
It's thickened and developed by
my kin. My clan. My tribe.

By the same days, by the same nights,
that shaped them, just as it shaped me.

Why do you blame the mango?
But not the mango tree?

Tolerated Acceptance

You boast of being kind,
a force to reckon with.
You boast of your forbearance,
and your abundant patience.

Will you tolerate my bold visions?
My perceptions of lost causes and actions?
Of songs unsung,
because they would be tolerated by no one?

You tolerate me.
But I accept you,
wholeheartedly.
Undoubtedly.

Fallen Branches

Death is daring. So covetous. So devious.
It claims precious souls of the living,
amidst the grieving.

This disease is Death itself.

Unsuspecting. Always traveling
amongst unsuspecting travelers.
Waiting to be reunited with its host, like lost lovers.

The branches from the family trees,
fall one by one.
No matter whether they believe,
that Death will finally take leave.

Towering smoke continues to tower,
as worlds burn, and the graves get deeper.
Branches to burn the bodies.
More branches fall off the family trees.

Branches to rest the barely living.
Fallen branches,
as far as the misty eyes can see.

My Prayer For You

I do not know
whom to pray to.
I do not know
if my prayers will be answered.

I do not know if you know
that my prayers
are prayers,
said religiously for you.

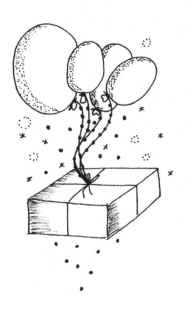

Sweaty Palms

A new endeavor.

You thought of something clever.

You must contain the excitement. The fever,

that is rising from knowing,

that you're about to uncover,

something unheard of. Oh, how clever!

Sweaty palms.

It's your body's way of staying calm.

So that the others can't tell,

that you're trembling. That you're trying

not to shriek in delight.

Sweaty palms.

So that the others can't tell,

that you have no clue.

Yet somehow on the surface,

you appear to be the go-to.

Aging Together

Their paths
momentarily aligned,
with the stars,
and the Sun,
in the background.
It was quite the sight.

"You haven't aged a day."
said the Earth with a tired smile.

The Moon responded in shock,
"My Love, what have they done to you?!"

Mirror, Mirror

How much longer
will she stand in front of me?
Robed. Disrobed. Layered. Plain.
The usual turns.
Side. Front. Side. Back again.

How much longer
will she hide behind her skin?
But turn to me her mirror,
for validation?

If only she could see herself
through my eyes.
If only she believed,
that I cannot lie.

Justice Is Blind

Justice is blind.
And yet,
judges and juries
craft verdicts,
with doubtful eyes.

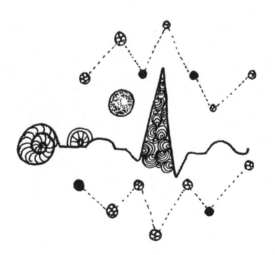

In The Eyes Of The Butterfly

Does the butterfly
believe in reincarnation?
Or does it feverishly soar high
believing that life always began,
as a butterfly?

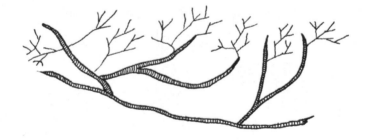

The Other Forms Of Privilege

Not struggling,

with sending a condolence message,
with the loss of family or friends,
to hold the arms that hold you,
to get out of bed,
with being at home,
with being alone,

is also called privilege.

Dear Ex And Foe

Dear Ex and Foe,
I'm sorry we parted the way we did.
It was needed for us to grow.

It was needed for us to heal.
For us to know what was real.

Dear Ex and Foe,
we were once friends.
This is how I choose to remember you,
until the bitter end.

A Girl's Journey

A boy and a girl.
Two children with different childhoods.
One has time to become an adult.

The other has no choice but to grow up,
and be tossed by a catapult
into a different reality.

"Mama...
You said I should be proud.
My body has matured and yet,
you look concerned and so full of doubt.
... are those happy tears, Mama?"

The Writer's Stories

They ask me where I get my stories from.
How far I must travel. How many languages I must speak.

Truth be told, I don't go very far. These stories come to me.
People known and new come to me with the desire,

to be heard. To be reassured,
when they can't swallow what they have chewed.

They come to me when they have given up.
When they want to speak their minds and empty their cups.

With their confessions. With their thoughts.
Reaching for articulation.

They come to me,
with the stories of their creation.

Parting Thoughts

Dear cartographers.
Fellow map makers.
Trackers of new horizons.
Scouts seeking new lands.

Your journey is your own,
and so is your map.
Detours. Diversions.
An incredible number of turns.

Know that with time,
your map will change.
And just like time,
no two destinations are ever the same.

Be curious.
Be kind.
Know when to stay,
and know when to walk away.

- Your fellow traveler,
Judy R. Sebastian

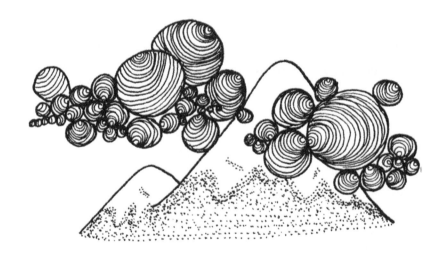

Meet Judy R. Sebastian

Judy R. Sebastian is a writer, speaker, and self-taught artist based in Oregon, United States. She is a Keralite who grew up in Dubai and is a third-culture individual. She started illustrating at the age of four and writing at the age of seven. Her mixed heritage strongly influences her artistic expression. Judy's career path is bifurcated and she serves her community as a Biotechnologist, Organizational Culture Consultant, Writer, and Artist – in no specific order. Through her work, she explores important social themes such as personal identities, adult learning, trauma, recovery, inclusion, equity, mental health awareness, and human rights. *Incomplete Maps* is the debut collection of poetry written and illustrated by Judy R. Sebastian. She hopes to inspire other people to experience the joys of self-discovery, self-forgiveness, self-healing, and self-love.

@judyrsebastian

www.judyrsebastian.com

INCOMPLETE MAPS

Every story begins with a blank page.

This is your space to share your tale.

Write away. Write your heart out.

If you'd like to share them with me,

use #incompletemaps or tag @judyrsebastian

Made in the USA
Coppell, TX
01 August 2021

59806999R00085